NATIONAL GEOGRAPHIC

Ladders

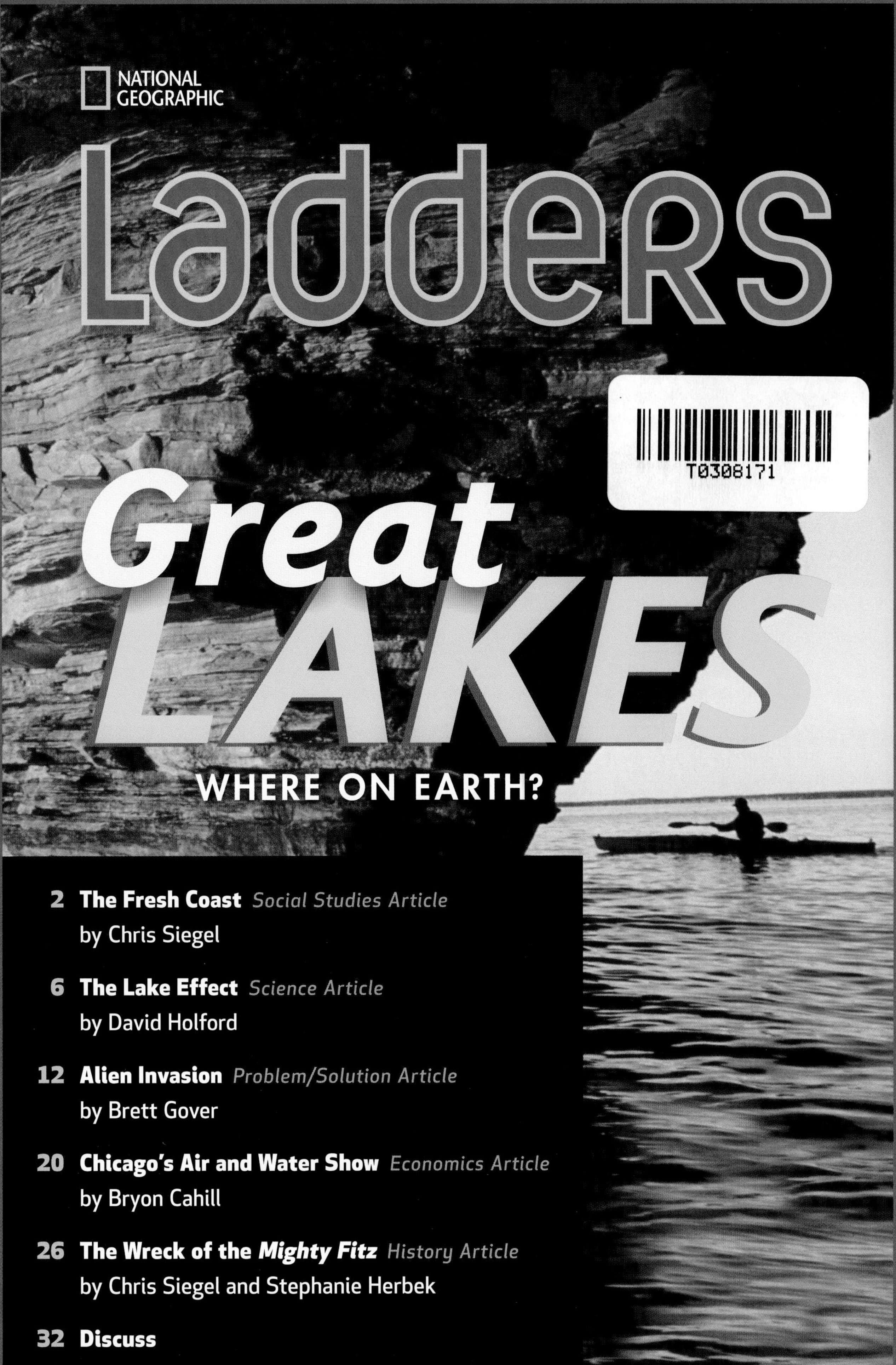

Great LAKES

WHERE ON EARTH?

GENRE Social Studies Article **Read to find out** about the geography of the Great Lakes.

The Fresh

by Chris Siegel

Have you been to Lake Superior, Lake Michigan, Lake Huron, Lake Erie, or Lake Ontario? These are the five Great Lakes. What makes them so great? These lakes are huge! If you stand on one side of any of them, you will not be able to see across to the other shore. These lakes are in the Great Lakes **basin** in the center of North America. They are in both the United States and Canada. A basin is like a shallow bowl. The sides are sloped so water drains toward the center. The lakes have many **tributaries**, or connecting rivers and streams. Together, the lakes and their tributaries have the largest amount of fresh water on Earth.

People have lived along the Great Lakes for thousands of years. The lake water has been used for drinking, fishing, and moving from place to place. The Great Lakes also help move goods around the world. Rivers and canals connect these lakes to the Atlantic Ocean. Cargo ships from Europe can reach Chicago, Illinois.

Miners Castle on Michigan's Upper Peninsula is part of Lake Superior's more than 2,700 miles of shoreline.

Coast

Where on Earth?

THE GREAT LAKES

Scientists study satellite photos to learn about the Great Lakes. These photos are taken from space. They help scientists learn how each lake changes over time. Slow-moving glaciers carved out valleys and made deep, hollow areas on Earth between 1.6 million and 10,000 years ago. Later, the area got warmer. The glaciers began to melt. This melting water filled in the hollow areas and formed the Great Lakes. Each lake has its own shape and size. Read more about each lake here.

Lake Huron

Average Depth: 195 ft.

Lake Huron has 30,000 islands. One is the world's largest freshwater island. It has a lake on it. And that lake has an island in it!

It is second largest by area, about the size of West Virginia.

A drop of water stays in Lake Huron for 22 years. That is how long it takes the lake to refill with all new water.

If the lakes look funny to you in this image, remember that a satellite can take a photo from many different angles. In this satellite photo, Lake Superior is at the bottom rather than on the left, where it appears on a map. But if you turn a map of the Great Lakes on its side so that Lake Superior is at the bottom, you'll be able to tell how the satellite was turned when it took this photo from space.

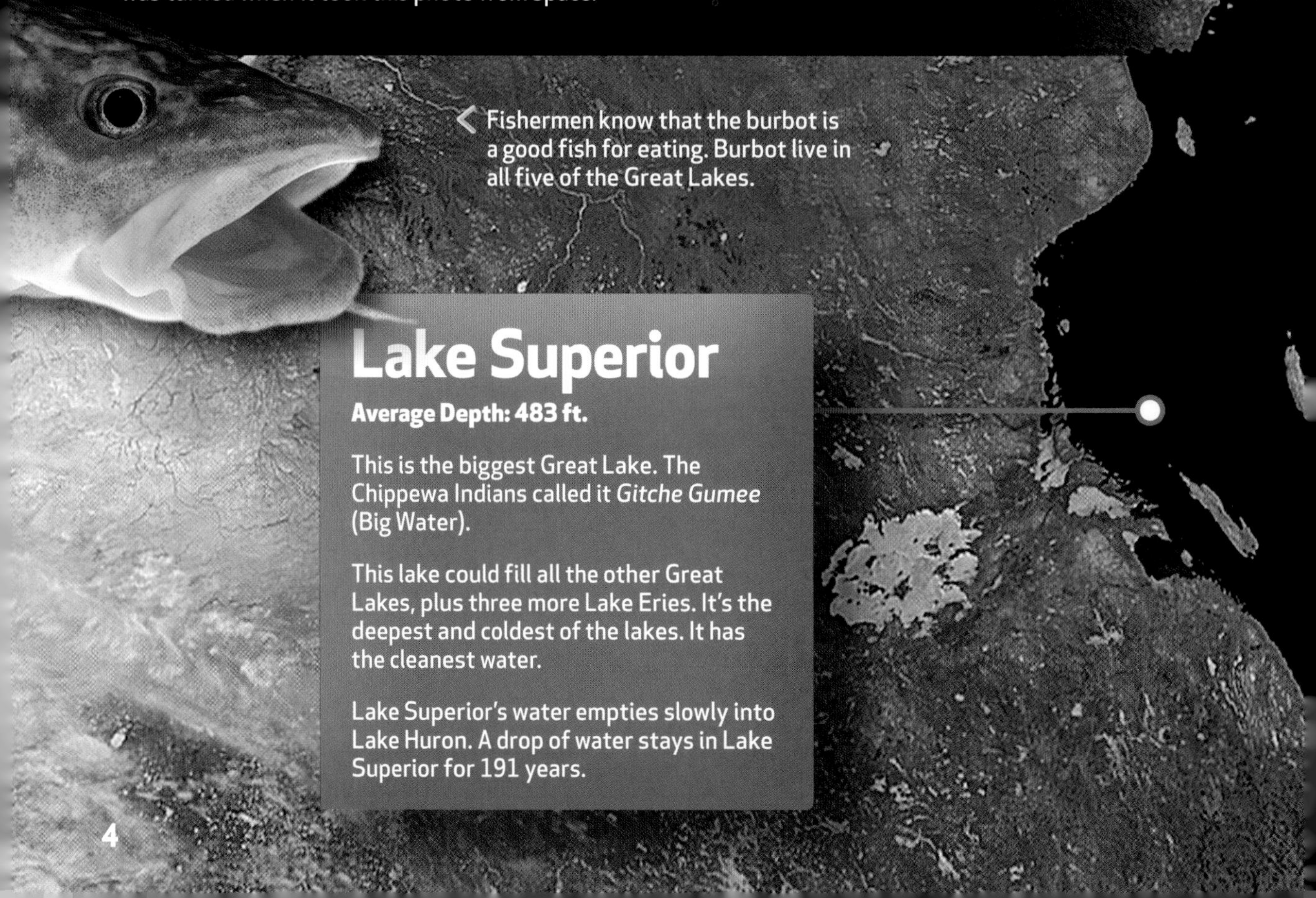

Fishermen know that the burbot is a good fish for eating. Burbot live in all five of the Great Lakes.

Lake Superior

Average Depth: 483 ft.

This is the biggest Great Lake. The Chippewa Indians called it *Gitche Gumee* (Big Water).

This lake could fill all the other Great Lakes, plus three more Lake Eries. It's the deepest and coldest of the lakes. It has the cleanest water.

Lake Superior's water empties slowly into Lake Huron. A drop of water stays in Lake Superior for 191 years.

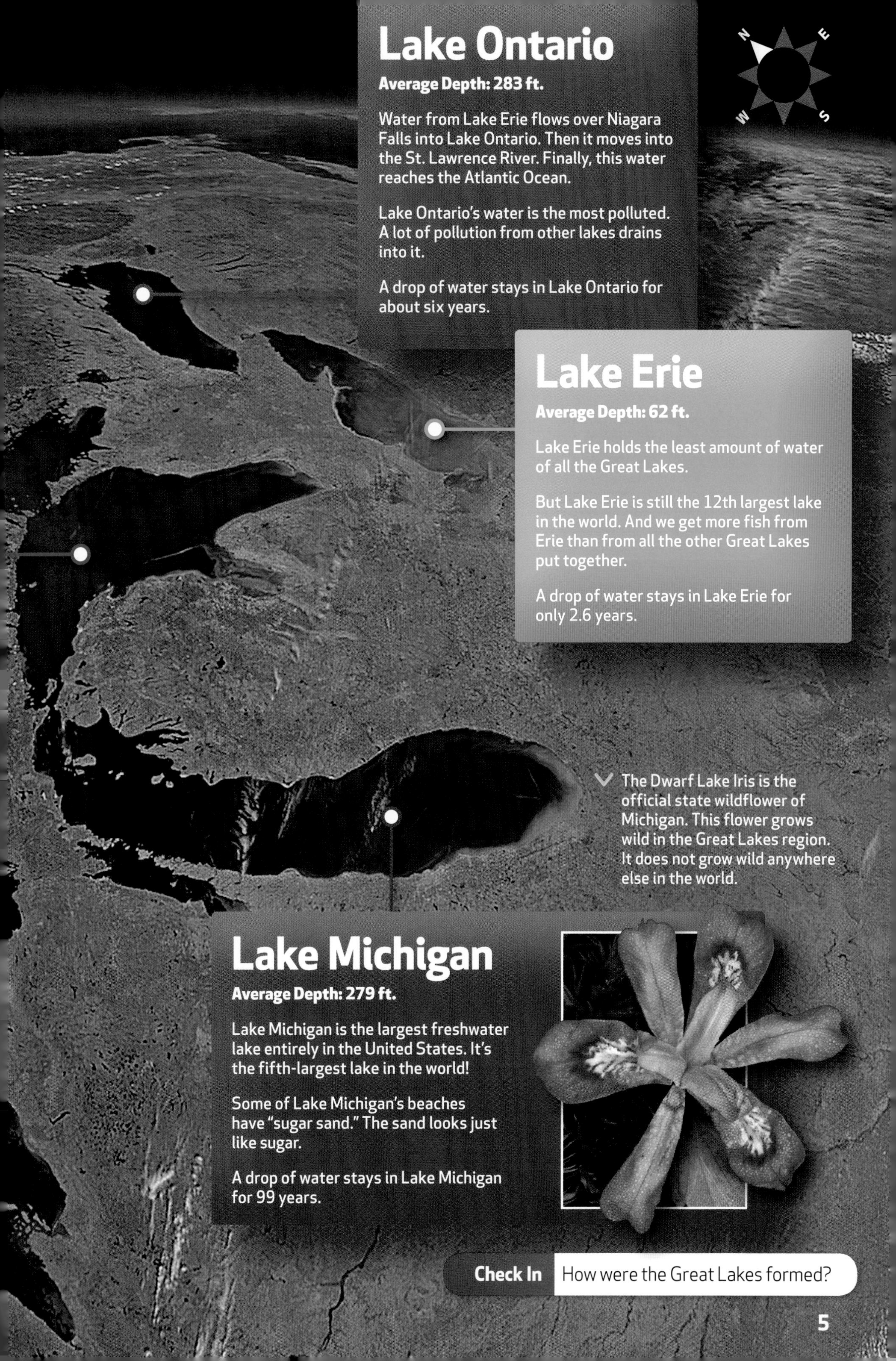

Lake Ontario

Average Depth: 283 ft.

Water from Lake Erie flows over Niagara Falls into Lake Ontario. Then it moves into the St. Lawrence River. Finally, this water reaches the Atlantic Ocean.

Lake Ontario's water is the most polluted. A lot of pollution from other lakes drains into it.

A drop of water stays in Lake Ontario for about six years.

Lake Erie

Average Depth: 62 ft.

Lake Erie holds the least amount of water of all the Great Lakes.

But Lake Erie is still the 12th largest lake in the world. And we get more fish from Erie than from all the other Great Lakes put together.

A drop of water stays in Lake Erie for only 2.6 years.

The Dwarf Lake Iris is the official state wildflower of Michigan. This flower grows wild in the Great Lakes region. It does not grow wild anywhere else in the world.

Lake Michigan

Average Depth: 279 ft.

Lake Michigan is the largest freshwater lake entirely in the United States. It's the fifth-largest lake in the world!

Some of Lake Michigan's beaches have "sugar sand." The sand looks just like sugar.

A drop of water stays in Lake Michigan for 99 years.

Check In How were the Great Lakes formed?

GENRE **Science Article** **Read to find out** how the Great Lakes influence the weather.

The Lake Effect

by David Holford

A winter storm is brewing over Lake Superior's Upper Peninsula. This area of the country gets lots of lake-effect snow.

It's exciting to look outside and see mounds of snow piled high on the ground. A "**lake-effect**" storm has brought 18 inches of snow!

Many people living near the Great Lakes have to deal with the lake effect. This is how a large lake affects weather in places nearby. The most extreme lake effect is lots of snow.

In winter, the air around the lakes cools faster than the water in the lakes. Cold air blows over the lakes. The air pulls warmth and moisture from the water. Clouds form. Once the warmed air hits land, it cools again. Then moisture in the clouds falls as snow.

The winds that cross the Great Lakes come from the northwest and Canada. So the areas south and east of the lakes get the most snow. These areas of heavy snowfall form a **snowbelt**.

As Earth slowly becomes warmer, more lake-effect snow will fall. That's because it will take longer for ice to form on the Great Lakes in winter. Less ice means warmer water. And that brings more snow. Syracuse, New York, is in the snowbelt. It's getting 50 percent more snow per year than it did 100 years ago.

Ice collects along the Lake Superior shoreline in Ontario, Canada.

Snow Day

Hold a yardstick beside you. Add seven inches to the top. Now imagine that much snow! In early December 2010, more than 43 inches of snow fell on Syracuse. Snow fell for four days. During the worst of the storm, as much as two inches of new snow fell each hour. Dozens of schools closed.

This wasn't the only snowfall in Syracuse that month. More snowstorms followed. By December 21, six feet of snow had fallen on this snowbelt city.

Syracuse has averaged about ten feet of snow per year since 1951. Lake Erie and Lake Ontario cause this lake-effect snow to fall across the snowbelt in western New York. But most Syracuse residents are used to this extreme weather. The snowstorm of 2010 didn't slow the city down for long. Schools were only closed for two days.

A family pitches in to clear snow from the street after the December 2010 Syracuse snowstorm.

The winter of 2010–2011 was one of the snowiest in Syracuse history. This photo shows snow falling in Clinton Square in downtown Syracuse. In total, Syracuse received nearly 15 feet of snow that winter.

People enjoy cool breezes and sunny skies at Chicago's North Avenue Beach. This popular beach is located on the shore of Lake Michigan.

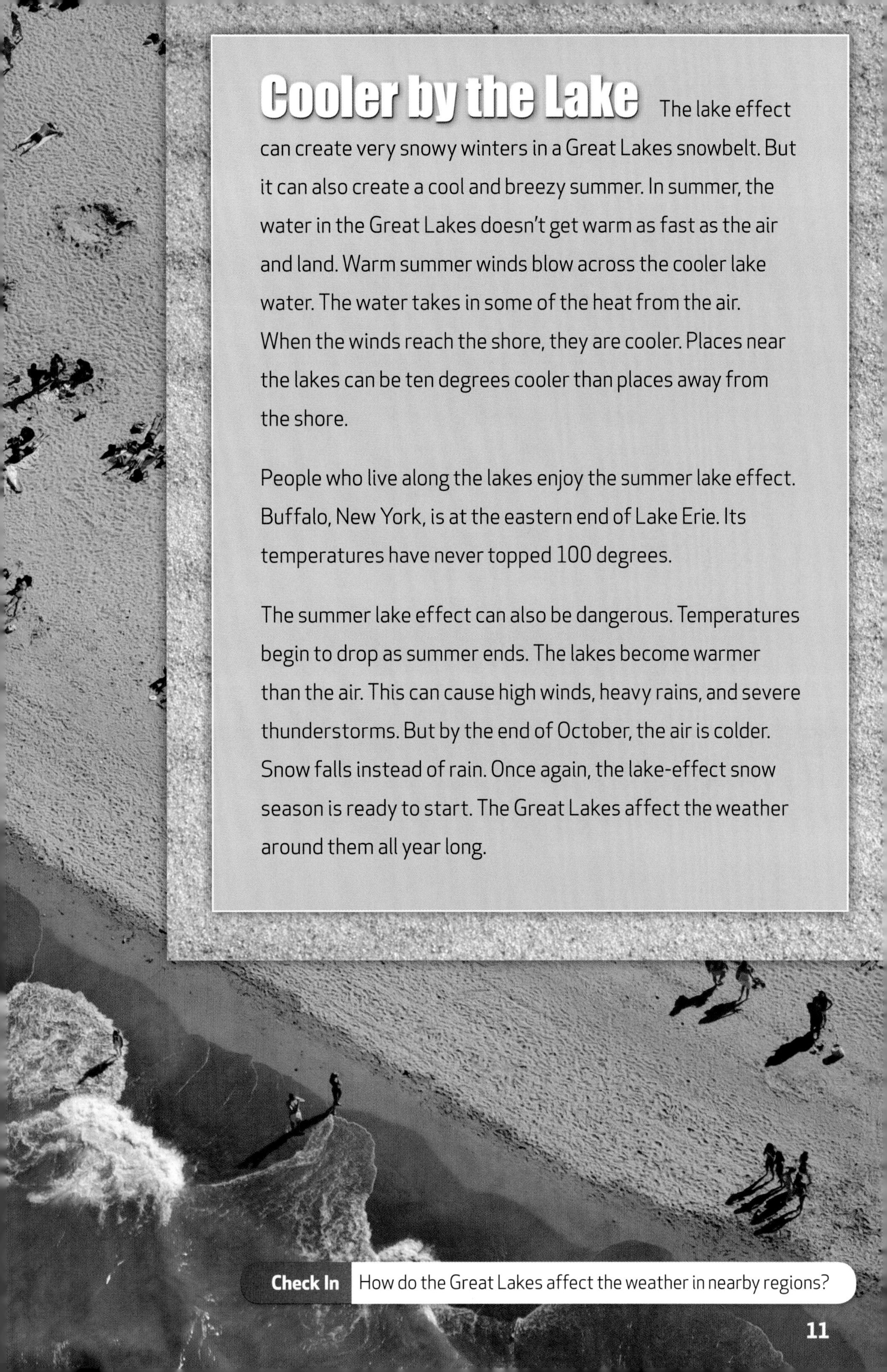

Cooler by the Lake

The lake effect can create very snowy winters in a Great Lakes snowbelt. But it can also create a cool and breezy summer. In summer, the water in the Great Lakes doesn't get warm as fast as the air and land. Warm summer winds blow across the cooler lake water. The water takes in some of the heat from the air. When the winds reach the shore, they are cooler. Places near the lakes can be ten degrees cooler than places away from the shore.

People who live along the lakes enjoy the summer lake effect. Buffalo, New York, is at the eastern end of Lake Erie. Its temperatures have never topped 100 degrees.

The summer lake effect can also be dangerous. Temperatures begin to drop as summer ends. The lakes become warmer than the air. This can cause high winds, heavy rains, and severe thunderstorms. But by the end of October, the air is colder. Snow falls instead of rain. Once again, the lake-effect snow season is ready to start. The Great Lakes affect the weather around them all year long.

Check In How do the Great Lakes affect the weather in nearby regions?

GENRE Problem/Solution Article

Read to find out how invasive species affect the Great Lakes.

ALIEN

Huge snakes called Burmese pythons slither across the Florida Everglades. They feast on native animals. In London, noisy ring-necked parakeets eat from fruit trees and bird feeders. They leave little food for native birds. In Cuba, a woody weed called *marabu* can grow ten feet high. It turns farmland into thorny jungles.

What do the pythons, parakeets, and woody weeds have in common? They are **invasive species**. These species are not native to the **ecosystem** in which they are found. They can harm the environment.

Invasive animals compete with native species for food, space, and other resources. They usually have no **predators**, or animals that hunt and eat them. Their

Asian carp are known for their large size. They also have an incredible leaping ability.

INVASION

by Brett Gover

numbers grow quickly. Soon they begin crowding out the native species.

How do invasive species get to their new ecosystems? Some are carried from their native ecosystems to new ones. This can happen by accident. For example, a seed can be carried from one place to another on a ship. Other times, it happens on purpose. People bring species from one place to another. They hope the new species will get rid of a pest or solve a problem.

There has been an explosion of invasive species. In the United States, the Asian carp has invaded the Mississippi River system. This large fish now threatens to enter the Great Lakes. How did this happen? What might happen next? Let's find out.

THE INVASION BEGINS!

In the 1970s, fish farmers and government agencies wanted to keep the water in their ponds and lagoons clean. They hoped Asian carp would solve this problem. They brought Asian carp to the United States on purpose. These fish eat tiny plants and animals that make the water look dirty.

Fishermen are often amazed at the size of the Asian carp they pull in. There are no freshwater fish in North America big enough to eat an adult Asian carp.

Then floods hit. Some of the carp swam into nearby streams that flow into the Mississippi River. The carp began to spread through the Mississippi and its smaller branches, or tributaries.

Many people are concerned. The numbers of Asian carp keep growing. These fish are big and strong. They grow up to five feet long and can weigh more than 100 pounds.

Asian carp can leap ten feet out of the water. This can harm boaters. But Asian carp pose an even bigger danger.

TAKING OVER

Asian carp eat tiny animals and little plants called algae. But they have huge appetites. They eat the food that other fish need. The other fish don't get enough food and begin to die off.

The fish that are left have to compete against the Asian carp. Asian carp can produce hundreds of thousands of eggs at a time. So their numbers can grow very fast. Young carp grow quickly, too. They soon become so big that no other fish prey on them.

OTHER INVADERS

Dozens of other harmful species have already invaded the Great Lakes. Read the photo captions to learn about a few of these species.

Sea lampreys are the vampires of the Great Lakes. They have long bodies like eels. Their mouths are like suction cups. They attach themselves to fish and suck their blood. The victims often die. In this photo, sea lampreys attach to a brown trout.

The longer the Asian carp live in an area, the more they take over. They crowd out the native fish.

Asian carp have now taken over much of the Mississippi River system. In Illinois, they're within a few miles of Lake Michigan. Experts fear that if they get into the Great Lakes, they could wipe out many native fish species. This would ruin the fishing industry and greatly harm the Great Lakes ecosystems.

The tiny shellfish called zebra mussels cluster in huge colonies. They block water pipes at power plants and water treatment facilities. They damage boats, piers, and buoys.

Purple loosestrife can grow up to seven feet tall. It can produce several million seeds a year. This plant spreads and crowds out native plants along the marshy shores of the Great Lakes.

ALIEN SPECIES: KEEP OUT!

The Asian carp invasion is a tricky problem. There are a few possible solutions, but none of them is perfect.

Near the southern tip of Lake Michigan, **canals** link the Mississippi River system to the Great Lakes. A canal is a human-made waterway. The canals are the easiest path for Asian carp to reach the lakes.

Engineers are trying to stop the carp. They've put electrical barriers in the canals. When fish come near the barriers, they feel a shock and swim the other way. But if the carp get through the barriers, they could spread quickly. Is this the best solution? Read more and decide for yourself.

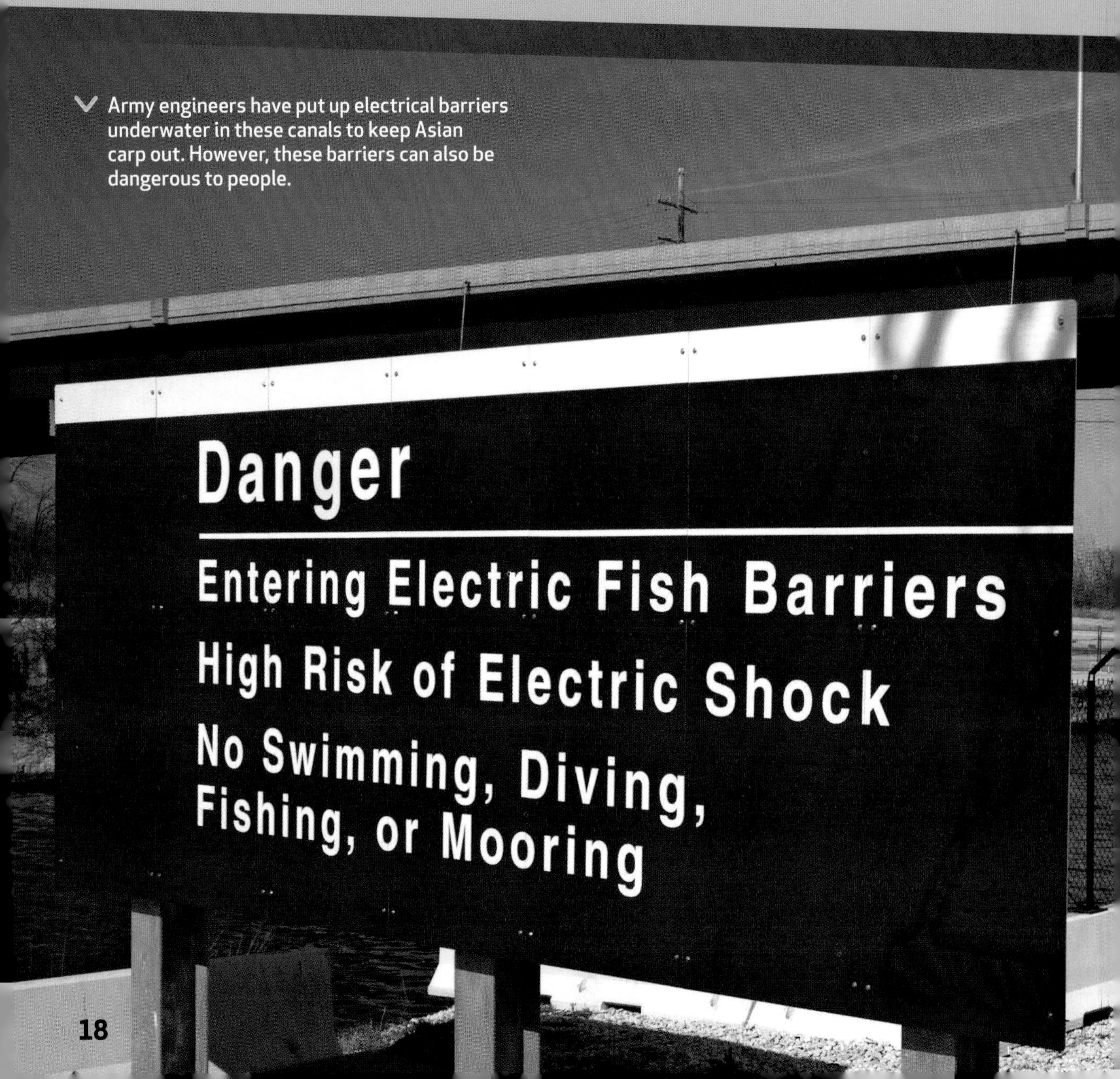

Army engineers have put up electrical barriers underwater in these canals to keep Asian carp out. However, these barriers can also be dangerous to people.

SOLUTION 1:

Electric barriers have been installed 50 miles from Lake Michigan. This seems to be working so far. Only a few carp have been found between the barriers and Lake Michigan, and they were removed. But the barriers are costly. Plus, if they ever lose their electric current, the Asian carp will be able to swim right into the lakes.

SOLUTION 2:

Another solution is to close off the canals from the Mississippi River system. Closing the canals might stop Asian carp from entering the Great Lakes. But ships use these canals to travel from the Great Lakes into other bodies of water. Closing the canals would make it difficult to move goods throughout the country.

WHAT DO YOU THINK?

Many people are worried about Asian carp getting into the Great Lakes. Are electric barriers the answer? Should we close off the canals? We need to find the right solution and act on it in time.

^ The Mississippi River is more than 150 miles from the western shore of Lake Michigan. Yet it is connected to the lake via the Illinois and Des Plaines Rivers, and then a series of canals. The carp barrier shown on this map helps stop carp from moving from the Mississippi River system to the Great Lakes.

Check In What could happen if Asian carp get into the Great Lakes?

GENRE Economics Article

Read to find out how Great Lakes tourism can benefit local communities.

Chicago's Air and Water Show

by Bryon Cahill

VROOM! A loud roar fills the air above Lake Michigan. Six jets swoop down, leaving trails of white smoke behind. The jets twist and turn through the air.

The jets fly in a diamond-shape formation. They are close together, sometimes only 18 inches apart. It's a thrilling sight!

Chicago's Air and Water Show brings more than 1.5 million people to the area each year. It encourages **tourism**, which is good for Chicago

Pilots practice their stunts before the show in the air above Chicago's lakefront.

businesses. People spend their money in restaurants, hotels, and stores. Tourism provides jobs and money to Chicago. This boosts the city's **economy**, or the money and goods that come into and go out of a community.

Chicago's Lake Michigan shore is the perfect place for the oldest free air and water show in the United States. The lake waters stretch east. This gives planes a large, safe flying area. And Chicago's beaches, parks, and harbors stretch far north and south. This gives all viewers a place to watch the show.

The Show Takes Off

This event began in 1959 with a budget of only $88. It was a small celebration for children in a Chicago day camp. The event included water ballet, water skiers, and a diving contest. The Coast Guard also showed how to rescue someone from the lake in a helicopter.

Crowds can view impressive sights in both the water and the sky.

The Air and Water Show has become bigger every year since. In 1960, the U.S. Army Air Force Thunderbirds performed for the first time. They zoomed, dove, and rolled through the sky. The U.S. Army Golden Knights Parachute Team also jumped into the skies over Chicago that year. They plunged down into the waters of Lake Michigan.

Today's Air and Water Show viewers are still impressed by amazing sights. A helicopter rolls and flips through the air. It even turns upside down! Its daredevil pilot is one of only three pilots in the world with a license to perform these stunts.

The audience keeps cool in Lake Michigan while watching daredevil pilots perform amazing stunts.

A member of the U.S. Navy Parachute Team lands in front of a packed crowd. The team is known as the "Leap Frogs."

The Wild Blue Yonder

Some of the popular performers return each year. Today's Air and Water Show still features parachute jumpers. They jump from 12,500 feet in the air. And the Coast Guard still gives a search-and-rescue demonstration.

Some years, the U.S. Army Air Force Thunderbirds are the main attraction. Other years, it's the U.S. Navy Blue Angels. The Blue Angels fly a F/A-18 Hornet aircraft. It can go up to 1,400 miles per hour (mph). That's twice the speed of sound! But that's too fast for the show. The pilots are only allowed to go about 700 mph. That's still more than ten times as fast as the average highway speed limit.

It takes years of training to learn how to fly these planes. Blue Angels pilots need at least 1,200 flying hours to make the team. The commanding

The Blue Angels' jets all carry the U.S. Navy's official colors—blue and gold.

officer of the Blue Angels needs at least 3,000 hours of training! The pilots love showing off their skills at the Air and Water Show. And every August, audiences pour into Chicago to see these amazing stunts.

The Blue Angels perform at many air shows. About 11 million people see them each year.

Check In How does the presence of the Air and Water Show affect the economy of Chicago?

 Read to find out about a famous Great Lakes shipwreck.

The Wreck of the Mighty Fitz

by Chris Siegel and Stephanie Herbek

The Great Lakes are some of the most dangerous waters on Earth. They can be difficult to **navigate**, or find one's way through. They are known for sudden storms and huge waves. These waves can sink a ship with little warning. That might be just what happened to the *Mighty Fitz*.

The S.S. *Edmund Fitzgerald*, or *Mighty Fitz*, was the largest carrier ship on the Great Lakes in 1958. It weighed 13,632 tons and stretched 729 feet long. It had carried more than a million tons of iron ore across the Great Lakes. But its final voyage began on November 9, 1975, in Superior, Wisconsin. Captain Ernest M. McSorley was at the helm.

The *Mighty Fitz* was traveling across Lake Superior when it met up with the S.S. *Arthur M. Anderson*. Both ships were headed for the Great Lakes steel mills. On November 10, 1975, a winter storm blew in. It had hurricane-force winds and waves up to 35 feet high. The *Mighty Fitz* disappeared into Lake Superior. It carried 29 crew members down with it.

This painting depicts the final voyage of the S.S. *Edmund Fitzgerald*. "S.S." stands for *steamship* in a ship's name.

NO CALL FOR HELP?

The *Anderson* and *Fitzgerald* kept radio contact throughout their voyage. Around 7:10 p.m. on November 10, a crewman on the *Anderson* radioed the *Mighty Fitz*. He received a brief response: "We are holding our own." The *Fitzgerald* disappeared from the *Anderson's* radar screen shortly after. It was never seen above water again. This is the radio transmission that took place between the crews on that fateful night.

Fitzgerald: Anderson, this is the Fitzgerald. I have sustained some topside damage. I have a fence rail laid down, two vents lost or damaged, and a list. I'm checking down. Will you stay by me 'til I get to Whitefish?

(checking down: slowing the ship's speed; list: tilt to one side)

Anderson: "Charlie" on that, Fitzgerald.

("Charlie": got it)

\# # #

Anderson: Fitzgerald, this is Anderson. Have you checked down?

Fitzgerald: Yes, we have.

Anderson: Fitzgerald, we are about 10 miles behind you, and gaining about one and a half miles per hour. Fitzgerald, there is a target 19 miles ahead of us. So the target would be nine miles on ahead of you.

(target: another ship)

Fitzgerald: Well, am I going to clear?

Anderson: Yes, he is going to pass to the west of you.

Fitzgerald: Well, fine.

Anderson: By the way, Fitzgerald, how are you making out with your problems?

Fitzgerald: We are holding our own.

(holding our own: doing OK)

Anderson: Okay, fine. I'll be talking to you later.

THE LAST VOYAGE OF THE *FITZGERALD*

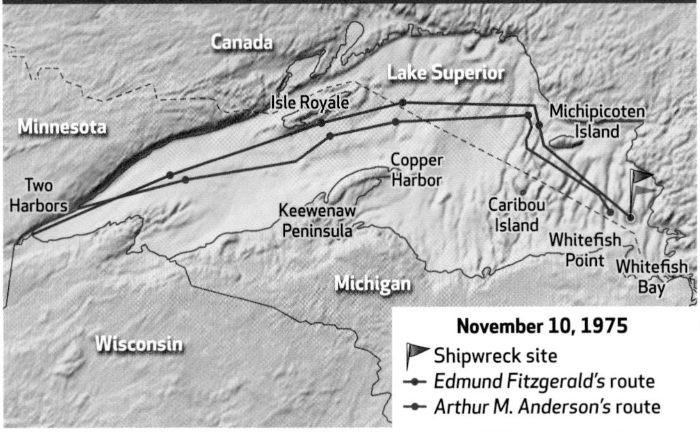

WHAT HAPPENED TO THE *MIGHTY FITZ*?

No **distress call**, or call for help, ever came from the *Fitzgerald*. This has baffled investigators for decades. The ship and its crew simply disappeared. Did the storm sink the *Mighty Fitz*?

The Great Lakes can be less safe for ships and sailors than the ocean. November is an especially dangerous month in this region. Moving goods across the Great Lakes is risky for ships. The *Mighty Fitz* was no exception.

What caused the shipwreck? Did the storm's high waves sink the *Fitzgerald*? Did the ship hit the bottom of the lake and break apart? The sinking remains a mystery.

THREE SINKING THEORIES

Both ends of the ship may have been pushed up by waves. The *Fitzgerald's* heavy cargo was located in the center of the ship. This could have caused the ship to crack in half.

"Three Sisters" are a series of three gigantic waves. They may have struck the *Fitzgerald*, flooding and sinking it.

The *Fitzgerald* passed a shallow area near Caribou Island. If the ship got too close, it may have "bottomed out," or hit the bottom of the lake in a shallow area, cracking on impact.

A diver inspects the wreckage of the *Edmund Fitzgerald*, more than 500 feet underwater.

REMEMBERING THE *MIGHTY FITZ*

The crew of the *Anderson* was worried when they lost contact with the *Fitzgerald*. Shortly after, they found two lifeboats and other **debris** floating in the water. There was no sign of survivors. Later, the Coast Guard looked for wreckage with planes, ships, and **sonar**. Two large pieces of debris were found. It was the *Mighty Fitz*.

Thousands of shipwrecks lie on the bottom of the Great Lakes. The front and back ends of the *Fitzgerald* are intact. The midsection is broken. The wreckage lies deep in Lake Superior in Canadian territory. Few divers have seen it, but better technology helps more people visit every year. The Canadian government limits those who can visit, out of respect for the lost sailors.

^ The ship's bell had water damage when it was raised from the wreckage. It was restored before being placed in the museum.

The *Fitzgerald's* 200-pound bronze bell was removed from the wreckage by the Great Lakes Shipwreck Historical Society in 1995. It was a joint effort between the National Geographic Society, Canadian Navy, Sony Corporation, and a Michigan tribe of Chippewa Indians. The bell is on display in the Great Lakes Shipwreck Museum in Michigan. It is rung 29 times—once for each lost crew member—on the anniversary of the shipwreck every year.

Check In What sequence of events led to the sinking of the *Fitzgerald*?

Discuss

1. What connections can you make among the five selections in this book? How do you think the selections are related?
2. Would you like to live in a region that had lake-effect weather? Why or why not?
3. What are some of the effects of invasive species on the Great Lakes?
4. Consider the three different theories that try to explain why the *Fitzgerald* sank. Which one do you believe is the best explanation for what happened? Why?
5. What do you still wonder about the Great Lakes and the issues that affect the region?